ASCLEPIAS:
THE MILKWEEDS

ASCLEPIAS: THE MILKWEEDS

Nathanaël

NIGHTBOAT BOOKS
New York

To Amina Cain
ami and friend

I could say of this book that its principal concerns are discrepancy, and extinction. But I would be suspicious of such a claim, and the person who made it.

Almost all the texts gathered in it were intended as talks, with few exceptions, and in addition to being written, most often in response to an invitation, were also spoken, in a room, before people, and at times in different languages. With the languages come cities, both proximate and removed (but in which sense are the vectors to be drawn, and how is one to uphold such distinctions ?).

Whatever their misdirection, the itineraries herein—all of which owe something to address— make clear the indisputably tendentious implication of intimacy in the workings of the world. To say what a world is would require recourse to vocabularies that escape me ; perhaps it is enough to say that it is nothing more or less than what disappears from it.

In this sense, *Asclepias* functions as a *hic jacet*, with every emphasis on the lies. It lays no claim to a void, but rather it imagines what a voice might be in the absence of a voice, and it does so in layerings of photographic and translative movements, seeing in each of these disaggregative tendencies which are not the simple reinforcement of forensic evidence, but rather a record of slight adjustments in light receptivity. One of their incongruities may be in their obstinate observation of solitude, a solitude that is in resolute contradiction with their incitements.

Perhaps I can put it this way : It happens that one is altered, at first, imperceptibly, by one's surroundings. The curtains are drawn for days at a time (though it may feel like months or years), and the eyes shut against the inexhaustibly insistent pangs of vitality. Until one steps into the air again to find things exactly as one had left them.

—Nathanaël
July 2014

Then he sees that the I is contained in the
world, and that there really is no I, and thus the
world cannot harm the I, and he calms down ;
or he sees that the world is contained in the I,
and that there really is no world, and thus the
world cannot harm the I, and he calms down.
And when man is overcome again by the horror
of alienation and the I fills him with anxiety,
he looks up and sees a picture ; and whichever
he sees, it does not matter, either the empty I
is stuffed full of world or it is submerged in the
flood of the world, and he calms down.

But the moment will come, and it is near, when
man, overcome by horror, looks up and in a
flash sees both pictures at once. And he is seized
by a deeper horror.

—Martin Buber
tr. W. Kaufmann

(Self-)translation
An expropriation of intimacies

It recently occurred to me while re-reading Buber's *I and Thou*—*Ich und Du*—which I was in fact not re-reading, since that would have meant poring over Walter Kaufmann's translation, but reading for the first time in G. Bianquis's French translation, *Je et Tu*, now exorbitantly out of print—and I just want to add that this decision to read German in French is already a form of disloyalty since it contravenes a sustained decision to read *as close* to the original as possible, thus, given the German and English languages' complicit antecedents, justifying such a practice, which this year suddenly seemed egregious to me (and only in the context of my very intimate relationship to these languages, all three of them, and not as broadly applicable, at all), which prompted me to deviate from this self-imposed norm, thus inviting further confusion into the transferences between languages, and further dislocation from the texts and authors in question, leading me to the realisation from which I have already multiply digressed, which is this : that contrary to the usual, perhaps even unusual, suggestion that translation offers the *closest possible reading of a text*, it may be that translation is in fact, may be, irreconcilably, disappointingly indicative of a *failure of reciprocity*. I will attempt, circuitously no doubt, to argue that this is not synonymous with its usual, very gendered, charge of disloyalty.

I should like to add also that this undecided decision, stemming from a misunderstanding or *malentendu*, is related to several significant events of the past few years, including a trip last November and December to Germany and

Austria, which I won't detail here, but want to
acknowledge as having been determining, in the
wake of the (last) months leading up to that trip,
in the realignment, or more aptly perhaps, the
deterioration of my existing geographies, as I had
hitherto come to understand them. In keeping
with an *understanding* of spacio-temporal rending,
I would add here to my lexicon the word
begreifen—this is, I promise, the only German
word I will mispronounce today, *heute*—to
grasp, and could sum up this interjection with a
stubborn surrender to *unbegreifen* or acatalepsy as
the murk encroaches on my thinking.

My geographies being inherent to my languages
and my body being ensnared in each, I will
eschew the inclination to make separate the very
ensconced Cartesian divide, and will borrow
instead from Claude Parent and Paul Virilio's
architectural vocabulary, to posit translation as
an *oblique* relationship, the oblique intimacies
of which entail the touching of texts in parts
and the gaping misalignments in others, the
partitioning of bodies of text precisely where they
touch, which is to say in *imperfect translation*,
in other words, catastrophically misaligned.
And to add here a delightful etymological
inconsistency : that to intimate may simultane-

ously indicate the covert (—or invert), explicit, communication of knowledge, *and* a declaration of war. As I write this, I have in mind Claude Cahun's photograph, *Que me veux-tu ?*, 1928, in which, doubly exposed, she looks accusingly at herself, and any number of Paul Virilio's photographs of the tilting bunkers which comprise the *Atlantikwall*. It is admittedly, an unusual architecture of bodies, a questionable landscape from which to think queerly about translation.

I said *invert*. It was and was not a slip of the tongue. What Claude Cahun accomplishes in this photograph, in which she *turns herself out*, is, for me, exemplary of the kinds of expropriations at work in the work of (self-)translation. Not every translation is a (self-)translation, and a (self-)translation need not necessarily concern the translation of one's own texts. Since 2006, I have been possessed and dispossessed by and of Claude Cahun, two photographs in particular, and the exegesis of this dispossession has resulted in several texts, each of which throws into question the location—the dislocation—of selves. Hers, and mine. This is in part due to the proliferation of selves in Cahun's work, also to the discomfiting resemblances between us, which I have considered at length elsewhere, to the historical (ethical) imperatives at work in her œuvre, and finally to the linguistic *indecision* surrounding this thinking, which has resulted in texts being shuttled back and forth between English and French, setting off a series of further inconsistencies (besides those which already inhabit each language distinctly), turning every point into a moving point and leaving none of the misdemeanists *answerable* for their delinquency.

Having elsewhere reserved the right to disloyalties of various kinds, and Cahun's work being exemplary of this, I am inclined (with Virilio and Parent) to approach the question of translation's misconduct from the point of view of estrangement, the very thing which arguably led me astray in the first place. (Astray, *l'égarement*, having wound its way, out of *L'absence au lieu*, into English, in *Absence Where As*, as *estrangement*, misaligning the versions but not, I am adamant about this, annulling one another, such that in this instance, *setting against* implies and implicates the literal co-existence of versions, which may or may not be capable of speaking to one another). It is here, perhaps that the German language enters into the very unstable equation being worked out : it is one which denies equivalency, and rebukes

verifiability. By setting German *against*, which
is to say along with and in contradiction to,
French, not only do several tremors begin to
destabilize the grounds upon which I am used to
working, but there is the occurrence also of a
concomitant elucidation of dis-temporalities,
which I am tempted to refer to as distempers. The
distinctions are so blatant that it is not possible
to be lulled into intimations of sameness, a
sameness which is nowhere evident, not even
in the sorts of proximities which may be present
between so-called Romance languages, or
Semitic languages, for example. And these are
not reducible either to considerations of accent
or gait.

When Kaufmann translates Buber's *it does
not help you to survive*, he is saying something
slightly different from Bianquis's *il ne fait rien
pour te conserver en vie*, which I would return
to English as *it does nothing to keep you alive*.
The literal life force in this phrase, the force
behind living is in one version *over life* (survive), in the other, it is a lateral exertion that
is suggestive of modern technologies of artificial
sustenance. To be kept alive is possibly to
live *at the mercy* of a dominant operative. To
survive is to stand over—a position contrary

to *understanding*, which is where we began, in *begreifen*. But as I haven't intelligible access to Buber's German, I will stop with this conjecture right now, and turn my avid attentions to a corollary question, that of hermaphroditism.

I imagine it unlikely to find Buber and hermaphroditism in a same text let alone a same sentence, but I am stubbornly disinterested in abiding by the capricious laws of intellectual filiation. So Buber is my conduit to the question of hermaphroditism by way of linguistic disjuncture—the unlikely pairing of a Saxon and Romance language out of which the tactile inconsistencies might bear out unusual textual pleasures and tensions. And it is this *it does not help you to survive* coupled with *it does nothing to keep you alive*, this slight differentiation, which slides the text a little to one side, such that superimposed, their juncture would result in a slur, a double-take, a stutter, a tribadic blur.

A blur is exactly where I might encounter hermaphroditism, or as I have written elsewhere, in another language, «Hermaphro*dite* est une parole désirée dans un corps inintelligible»—hermaphroditism is a desired word in an unintelligible body—here the English fails to convey the *dit* or dictum ensconced in the word *hermaphrodite*. And it may be that I could have foregone all that came before and simply presented you with this word and its embedded contradictions. Contradictions which are not the immediately apparent *hermes* coupled with *aphrodite* ; this contradiction is by now so customary that it hardly contravenes any of the rules of coupling, it disappointingly invigorates a particular binary. No, it is not this in *hermaphrodite* that enchants me, that bespeaks a *failure of reciprocity*, but its untransferrable unintelligibility. What it says, may say, in one language and not in another.

Syntactically speaking, the sex of the sentence is not (necessarily) transferrable. A body thus destabilised loses sight of its referent when transversing into another language. English's pronominal preoccupation, for example, singles out the subject's gender as part of speech, which in French, again for example, is severally located in the sentence. Where one benefits from the ambiguity the other falls into normality. To dislocate gender's stranglehold in French, one must strive for discord, grammatical disagreement in the place of English's mis-fitted neutering.

We are unforeseen and uncalled for. Hermaphroditism might be just that, a plunge into the
desiring body far from nominal preoccupations.
Masculine *and* feminine or rather neither, in
other words elsewhere, which for me is an act
of presence : *there*. Away from decided forms
of determined political discourse, but instead :
facing one another. This too is unintelligible. To
be caught off guard is nonetheless to give oneself
to the instant. The instant in its duration.

The failure of reciprocity is in this instance reciprocity's wager. To vigilate in the absence of one
another, two or more collateral texts, bespeaking
Buber's manifold insistence that "You cannot
come to an understanding about it with others".
It is this misunderstanding, this inability to
reciprocate, which enflames desire's hold. To say
"you" in text is to split the pronominal seam, to
make loyal this disloyalty.

April 2010

Vigilous, Reel
Desire (a)s accusation

Chaque fois, si fidèle qu'on veuille être, on est
en train de trahir la singularité de l'autre à qui
l'on s'adresse.

—Jacques Derrida

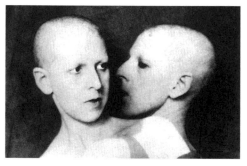

Que me veux-tu ? (1928)

J'ouvre et je vois, j'appréhende, ce qui de
moi n'est pas à moi et ne m'étant m'adresse
une réplique catastrophée. [1]

To speak at the last ; to take up speaking,
this that is in my throat, and to give it

---

[1] I open and I see, I apprehend, that which of me
is not mine and being not (of) me address myself a
catastrophied retort.

to the space just beyond the mouth, to push
past what resists speaking into address, a catch,
lurch into the blasted architecture of language's
predispositions, to speak, yes, say, to you, in
address, each, without recrimination, I am bereft,
not just, and unguarded, what *you* is spoken
out of me into a cataleptic reel, disallowed and
spleen, first, my disloyalties, and first again, in the
shrapnelled everlast, my culpability. § None of it
is unforeseen. What follows then is ever, always,
incomplete.

Desire's accusations are irrefutable. I come to
you with judgement and morbidity. Against
a theatre of moveable parts, Genet insists
"l'architecture du théâtre … doit être fixe,
immobilisée, afin qu'on la reconnaisse responsable : elle sera jugée sur sa forme." [2] This, then,

---

[2] *…the architecture of the theatre…must be fixed,
immobilized, so that it can be recognized as responsible :
it will be judged on its form.* Tr. Ch. Mandell. The full
passage in question reads : "Où aller? Vers quelle forme?
Le lieu théâtral, contenant l'espace scénique et la salle?
// Le lieu. À un Italien qui voulait construire un théâtre
dont les éléments seraient mobiles et l'architecture
du théâtre est à découvrir, mais elle doit être fixe,
immobilisée, afin qu'on la reconnaisse responsable : elle
sera jugée sur sa forme. Il est trop facile de se confier au
mouvant. Qu'on aille, si l'on veut, au périssable, mais
après l'acte irréversible sur lequel nous serons jugé, ou,
si l'on veut encore, l'acte fixe qui se juge."

is my injunction, that I bring with me, my "irreversible" theatre. § Judge me.

An "acte irreversible" may be a form of vigilance. An exacerbated attentiveness to vitality's decrepitude. § Surely, we are a wake, yes? The fantastical certitudes of presence are beguiling. But what of this : the torn-apart, seen, the over-seen and underwritten, they make perishable pledges. In the oxygenated body's (re)turn, there is already me against you against me : hard. Our vigilous turpitude.

It might be that in looking, the apprehensions are re-inscribed. *Re*, because the intimations, indeed the intimidations, precede us. We anticipate them, we make them. That we are. We imagine them imaginable. Imago, each, insect-like and sexable, you and me. Genet again : "l'acte fixe qui se juge." [3]

§ Fixe.
A form for looking, *je te fixe*, I stare at you. And if looking, *fixer, to stare, fixate*, is judgement, then this meeting is irrepressibly (ir)responsible. It is possible that these attentions that summon,

---

[3] *...the fixed act that judges itself.*

the manifestations of presence, in part, are
transliterations of belated, sometimes blatant,
violence. From mouth to morsel. Might we,
in keeping with our selves, do our best to fall
apart ? Our best kept. And sacrilege. § Lie to
me. Tell me what you want.

That form and act enact de-formity. It is this, I
think, that is a/e motion. With Buber, I concur,
emphatically : "it does not help you to survive." Is
that what we are here for ? Over-life ? (*Sur-vie ?*)
This is its disparity—and disparage. (Recalling
now that *parages* in French are the outskirts, the
outwards of a place, beyond a circumscribed area,
unmapped, but sensed, intimated, and it is this,
intimate, these intimacies, these topographical
skirtings which arouse my sensibilities, interpo-
late me overly : I go. *Dis*-paraging.)

§ Accusative. [4]
Lacan contends : "Le désir s'ébauche dans la
marge où la demande se déchire du besoin." [5]
Desire's recriminations reel. They are junctive
and enfold. If the body's edge is unintelligibly
marginal, then desire might be its marginalia—
sexed text. Whatever its outpouring, origination.
In an invented etymology of dis-parage, the act,
if this were an act with form—*begging judgement,*

responsibility—the act, then, would entail
the undoing (*dis*) of its sensed and sensory
outwards (*parage*) : its skin, if you will, peeled
back : flayed. § Is this what it is to be denuded—
proteus, of inconstant form—quickened?

These are desire's hermaphroditisms, counter-
sexed, unchecked, in pieces on the floor.
Demand rent from need makes a seam up the
middle of me. It is here that I mis-dream the
dream of what Buber calls "the double cry".
Echo ingested and thrown down, undaunted.
Woken, what sleeps, seeps from dream, de-
means : *Que me veux-tu ? What do you want
from me ?*

---

4 Accusative, a. 1. *Grammar*. In inflected languages
the name of the case whose primary function was
to express destination or the goal of motion ; hence
the case which follows prepositions implying motion
towards, and expresses the object of transitive verbs,
i.e., the destination of the verbal action ; sometimes
applied, in uninflected languages, to the *relation* in
which the object stands, as shown by its position
alone. By omission of the word *case, accusative* is
commonly used substantively. 2. (From ACCUSE
v.) Pertaining, tending, or addicted to accusation ;
accusatory. *Obs. rare.* (*Oxford English Dictionary
Online*, 2009.)

5 *Desire begins to take shape in the margin in which
demand rips away from need.* Tr. B. Fink.

There it is, demonstrably : demand ripped away
from need. In Claude Cahun's double exposure,
the twain self is put to the test of its (ir)revers-
ibility, face to face, conjunctive, obliterative
fixation : split at the point of seeing. What
vigil does (s)he keep ? Onanistic wounding, it
is the body severed from itself, re-joined, twixt,
tribadic, (s)he is all skin, undercut, misgiven.
Dualling herself. Here, in the locked-down
body-part, is the (im)parting of history that goes
ungiven, dis(ap)proving its acts.

§ Act.
Objection. Is equal parts objected and abjected,
simultaneous parsings of misspeaking. *Que me
veux-tu?* is already vanquished, exposure, its
architecture unconditionally disastered. *What do
you want from me* might be *want me* overturned,
veux on a verge of veulerie, accusing despondent
refusal, here, with me. A surge of deadliness, a
self with its sorrow rubbing the malignant parts,
propagating a heedless rush of disintegrations
which start small and become smaller and smaller
and more deadly, particulate. What sees seeing
is a morbid intimation, a cast-off accent, an
accident of being, where what passes passes on.
And we are (with) it. With : conjoined, vestigial.
In Cahun's splittings, reflective echoings of self

with self, this ontological distressor undresses the eyes that look not-looking. Our eyes, and it comes at me like this, with the full throttle of history slammed against an unprepared ground. If only it would shatter. If only it would bleed.

*

The conditional is bereaved : tense, unappeased. It carries potentiality's breach, boring into the undetermined with disbelief. The *if then* of me, constructed such that uncertainty, embedded in the causal palate of language's misdeed, is militantly rejected by a structuring of sated need. It locks into place, but this does nothing for a body that falls from a sky. The contaminant is alive, it is vital, distressed ; it disregards our posturings. "Rien n'est vrai", contends Édouard Glissant, "tout est vivant". It is this untrue-alive, which is the end of I (*je*)—its everlast. The insistence of Cahun's intransigent interrogation, speaking, alive : what want and to what end this accusation of endings? Each thing in ending, at the very start. It is sometimes called : onset. And we are its disease.

Cioran calls it fear : "La peur de la mort n'est que la projection dans l'avenir d'une peur qui

remonte à notre premier instant". "Le mal," he
insists, "le vrai mal est pourtant *derrière*, non
devant nous." [6] *Le mal* is also malady, affliction.
It touches the last in anticipation, it staggers
at our outwards, screwing the self to its ghastly
(dis)appearance. This is not timorosity—unless
it is a permeated vocable, with its suggestions
of rashness (*temerousness*), gravity (*morosity*)
and insistence (*temerity*) ; it is what it calls up
without speaking a word. Cahun's photographic
vigil is death's abandon, the halting of temporal
extravagance ; it is neither beginning's end, nor
end's beginning, but the monumental ripping
apart of history's seams, seemingly : a catastrophic
forethought unwound in the body's appellate
appeal. Death's unwieldy divide.

Unchaste it bemoans its (mis)demeanor. The
clasped features pursed at the threshold of an
imperilled, contrary kiss : might this be its
admission? § If we come running, it is to see past
the lurch of the thing coming at us, past mirror,
ill-reflected, concomitant sequence of disappearance, in which the photograph *reproduces*

[6] *Fear of death is merely the projection into the future
of a fear which dates back to our first moment of life.
Yet evil, the real evil, is behind, not ahead of us.*
Tr. Richard Howard.

what it rebukes, forcing it out of itself, unquelled
fornicant. What doesn't last, mimicry of a kindred,
menacing other-kind. Replica, a falsehood,
which begs the French *réplique*, the aftershock
of a kind of speaking, on a stage, in a residual
theatre : the re-hearsals of repetition (practice),
in which the manifold face is disregarded, and its
traits. Viscera.

At the point of suture, breasts striking one
another, clavicles fastened, thighs sewn to groin,
bones grafted together, something incoheres.
I want to say *self*, the (un)(m)asked *je*, in
ambiguity, but it is in the mouth, I hear it, the
mouth, in speaking, jeers. *Que me veux-tu?*
rips it apart. The melded together form is an
amorous atrocity. Think past the raced two-
backed beast ahead to Mengele's stitchings,
botched clonings, the quiet explosions in
each carcinogened throat. This too is closed.
Closed against a century come screeching to
a shrapnelled halt. It is from this that we are
thrown up, detritus, up-heaval, and this is as
I look back. Celan made it that far, tracking
language's fission, the determined destruction
of speech, perenially unwitnessed, obliviated,
still. Demanding : "Speak, you also, / speak as
the last, / have your say. // Speak— / But keep

yes and no unsplit". [7] Unsplit—negation and acquiescence, act and form, judgement and responsibility, speaking and seeing : twice swallowed back, twice more.

Unsplit—fissive—is Cahun's duplicitous duplication. *Que me veux-tu?* is the resilient outwardness of the *moi-je*, its act of aggressive fortress, the imparting of its grievance : this too is (un)given. An introverted address, delivered against a self of severalness. Here (in the body), the accusative other is a surrogate admonishment. The speaking to-against self is menially obliterative—self-speaking for self-seeing in history's optic disallows an iteration other than grief's opportunism : the self-same is the having been. It calls out its lastness, makes itself echo and chamber, absorbing shadow into shadowy light : "where death is ! Alive !"

If it is true that "Le désir est mort, tué par une image," [8] it may be that this accusatively emphatic image bespeaks the murderous vigil ; to watch, unbidden. To bring the body, unworn, to testify against itself, to make responsible its

[7] Tr. Michael Hamburger.
[8] Marguerite Duras. *Desire is dead, killed by an image*.

enmity, build up the wall of its own figuration,
severely, make what is seen visible against
history's rent screen—a black box of miserly
misery. Speak into speaking, unlistened. § I
go to where it happens. The door is a door
that closes. A gate that scrapes shut against a
forensic, vaulted compound. These are its barbed
technologies, its unmitigated heat, a fire that
doesn't burn, a blood that doesn't bleed : the
smell of it. If desire is dead it is dead at the point
of seeing, accused, beseeching. It dies undead, it
sees unspoken, it works its asphyxiation into the
endangered throat, stripped of its vital civility,
mouth open on no sound, untold. The wither
image may have killed desire, ineradicably.
Death's death as it were, remaindered at its
skinned edge, its posthumous (re)iteration, end
upon devastated end.

The photograph is fixed. It is what we see
Claude Cahun foreseeing, our looking back,
Orphic, and (s)he is beside herself. Fixed is
also contrived. It is volatility's compression,
the arrestation of dislocation. The fleeting self,
refined. Along with the rest of us, purged of our
purities. Our changeability is incumbent upon
it. There upon Genet's shattered columbarium
is ethics' structural impediment. The sanguine,

greedy respite from being. The graves he has us
digging (up). § I go there. I take you with me.
I wear it out. I wipe it back. I die your death.
With the mechanisms of futility. The egregious
armatures. A body carried out. *It* overtakes me.

*

This is address's vigil. Stood up against speaking,
the body closes its eyes against a fixed theatre
with its morbid charge of desirability. Our
reciprocal fixation is foregone. With martial
ease, when we meet. We are inseparable in our
imminence, and our defeat. *Que me veux-tu?*
realigns these empathic defections, forcing
agonic substance out, and the languages we
mis-speak. The blood of it is thick in me. With
you, I am suspect, here in this theatre.

November 2009

The tautological fury of a
disconsolate mind

(the present, dear friend, is there
a present, is it ever now?)

für John Beer, Philosoph

...nomme ici la philosophie : c'est l'anticipation soucieuse de la mort, le soin à apporter au mourir, la méditation sur la meilleure façon de recevoir, de donner ou de se donner la mort, l'expérience d'une veille de la mort possible, et de la mort possible comme impossibilité ;

...explicitly names philosophy : it is the attentive anticipation of death, the care brought to bear upon dying, the meditation on the best way to receive, give, or give oneself death, the experience of a vigil over the possibility of death, and over the possibility of death as impossibility.

—Jacques Derrida
tr. *David Wills*

, that I have given (to) the form of an
injunction : *nomme ici la philosophie*. Name
it. Stripped of its nominative clause, handed
to the immediate demand, the sentence,
hanged. Thus curtailed, philosophy's demonstrations are plied, *executed*, as it were, by
a syntactical constriction. Already I am in
the wrong, having wronged (a language).
The English makes clear indication of

my misdemeanour, disallowing the syncope that thwarted my initial reading. (I did not read the English translation, I referred to it). In the way that an unmemorable inscription—*To the memory of*—recently yielded the fantastical distortion,—*too much memory*—(a visual occlusion), the early moment of Derrida's sentence broke into my peering thus : *nomme ici la philosophie*. Name philosophy. Name it explicitly, to borrow from Wills' lexicon. Execute this act. As though the act of nomination were not in itself a violation of thought, a miscasting comprised of indefensible extrusions. Of murder, say it, murder. An injunction is also an enjoinder, its first demand is on, is of, is to : the present. Its principal subjugation is temporal. In principle, it summons time. Name philosophy : now. Nomination, which places one, *ipso facto*, in a critical state of abeyance or deferral in relation to naming itself, rends the very moment of naming, in a present convoked for the purposes of its undertaking, effectively tearing the mouth on the coordinates of (its) speaking. The appeal to tense is an avowal of syntactical misconduct, visited upon the sentence as it is unwritten in misreading, making demonstrable a mind's mis-take before the law of the letter. The imperative supplants the present indicative, disgorging the grammatical underparts, such that the disclosure of meaning is a disclosure first of the imposture of meaning ; an underhanded verdict, as it were, the sex hidden, exposed, its hiddenness exposed. The nominative injunction is foremost a possessive claim, pronominally predisposed. To make explicit the naming of this philosophy is to uncover the means of sexuation, to cast the face first as shadow, without consideration of the sun : to name, in other words to claim, the vigil by which the name becomes unpronounceable, in the forecasted death. Forecast in the present : capitulative copulative. Unpronounceable not for reasons of sacrality but of juridical furore : the pronouncement of a name is the pronounce-ment of a verdict, whose etymological substrata conjoin speaking to truth, yielding a veracity to nomination which naming ought to disallow. Such that a further dislocative reading of the truncated extract might train the disadvantaged eye to *grant philosophy its name, here* (ici), *in this place* implanting unwarranted generosity in the concurrent formulation. Collapsed away from habitual modes of intelligibility, the here may yet come to supplant the naming of philosophy altogether, such that the injunction *to name* dispossesses the namer of this force by furnishing the name to come : *name philosophy here*, give

philosophy this name : here, *ici*, and, implicit in
the imperative : *now*. The command bestows a
power that is incontrovertibly subdued, and the
addressee of this speaking, the feigned maker
of *verdict*, is rendered summarily speechless and
placeless, thus, perhaps, without a possible philosophy at present, without a possible present—
"heute nicht möglich"—*"impossible today"* [1]—
as though philosophy itself were dispossessed of
its present just as the present may not allow for
a philosophy, (*heute* and *Heute*, signifying, in
Bachmann's German, both today and the
present). Today's tautology is that it is foregone—"It merely signifies a day like all the rest";
undifferentiable, it is not situatable in time.
Such a temporal coordinate (*today*) signals
futility ; it announces its mortific inevitability
in the present in which it cannot subsist. To
command it is to admit defeat by it. Because
"today is a word which only suicides ought to
be allowed to use ; it has no meaning for other
people. It merely signifies a day like all the rest,"
philosophy's imperative is Sisyphean. There is
a concordance between *Selbstmörder* (suicides)
and *alle Anderen* (other people) in which the
murderous intent of language is made apparent ;

---

[1] Ingeborg Bachmann, *Malina*, tr. Philip Boehm.

this intent is the vector of its inexorability.
The inverse of death-giving in Derrida's French
(with intimations, in translation, of Celan's
death-bringing speech) is English's idiomatic life-
taking. Between the two, mouth and body are
indivisibly split. The tremor of being is the fatal
fault of ontological seismicity, in which each
human is strangled at birth, a rejoinder to their
subsistent mediocrity. Cioran's catapult away
from the moment of birth in favour of a drive
toward death evidences the redistribution of
vital energies. Neither limit allows for even the
postulate of consolation—this may be its ethical
bind ; to think thinking effectively requires the
removal of naming before even the occurrence of
a name : thought unthought—a residual equivocation with having never been. In the abstract
the suggestion of a void in the place of a self is
only effective if the self were never intimated
in the first place (un-born*e*) ; erasure is thus a
temporal impossibility, reliant, as it is, upon the
conditional—the requisition of the present.
In the desire for remove is an abhorrence of
repletion, a projection into vacuity. Philosophy's
donne (which is effectively a *done deal*) aggre-
gates something of Bachmann's *h/Heute* and of
Benjamin's *Jetztzeit* (now-time) ; it makes itself
annunciatory of a historical discrepancy between

temporality and existence, such that the present is ever, always, a present contingent on a kind of after-thought. The vigil of which Derrida's text is possessed can only be concerned with after, as a mode of attentiveness ; its *mot d'ordre* is too late.

[Il] voit passer l'ombre sur un verre dépoli du couloir. C'est vous, par le hublot. Vous êtes morte. [2]

[He] sees the shadow pass across some frosted glass in the passageway. It's you through the porthole. You are dead. [3]

[2] Pierre Jean Jouve.
[3] Tr. Lydia Davis.

+++++++++

Being Sisyphus

Sisyphus is still and always dead. The task of
reiteration to which he is assigned offers the
certitude of his having been. His presence is thus
substitutive : he holds his place. But Sisyphus
himself is foregone. The ever displacement of
the stone along the incline provides a remark-
able calculation of distances and degrees of
repetitive strain, but Sisyphus is in effect only
ever a shadow of Sisyphus. His toil instructs us
that *being* is only ever *after*. Camus's conclusion
that "Il faut imaginer Sisyphe heureux" (*One
must imagine Sisyphus happy*) is an enjoinder, a
plea, a perverse lament, and indicative of the
manipulations of the absurd upon thinking, or
of the absurd in thought. To think is to be
besieged ; to think with Sisyphus is to live in
conjunctive agreement with one's suicide, with
the tacit acknowledgement that the suicide of
Sisyphus is an undisclosed murder, with which
each is unavowably complicit.

December 2010

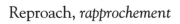

Reproach, *rapprochement*

J'ai besoin de catastrophes, de coups de théâtre.
—Hervé Guibert

With its vital concern for proximate
agonies, translation owes something
crucial to vigilation for its protean form.
If translation offers itself as literature's *wake*,
it is because it is already so suffused with
morbid abidance—it can only present itself
in catastrophic echo to what it might otherwise be. Which is to say that translation is
nothing other than the matter of death

itself, ruminated, deformed and devoured by its own attempts, verging on murderous complacency, duplicitous in its desiring. Mortific matter, as it were, immaterialised. Translation's *reproach*, then, which operates a paradoxical *rapprochement*, exists, of necessity, in the protraction of a work's cadaveric resistances. The deliberate misapprehension of these androgynous terms—reproach conjoined to *rapprochement*—make evident the untenable collusion between otherwise symbiotic signs. To near, in this instance, is to injure ; and injury, which is inimical to intimacy, takes the unexpected posture of an injunction.

*

If Hervé Guibert's *Le mausolée des amants* inflects Jean Genet's *strange word*,[1] it is precisely in its attentiveness to the necessary conjunction of death's exquisite theatre (the cemetery) to the city centre. Apprehensive,

---

[1] "L'étrange mot d'..." tr. by Charlotte Mandel as "That Strange Word." That strange word is of course "urbanism", but the titular ellipsis produces an ambiguity which leaves unresolved the presence of death in the city, or its imperative conjunction, as Genet would have it. To be conversant with the city is to be conversant with death ; the relational is thus of necessity inscribed with vital morbidity.

for the vitality of theatre, of the progressive removal of the cemetery from the urban clutch, Genet enjoins the *fixed act that judges itself*, gauging an architectural imperative for immobilisation. His impetus, an Italian theatre of moving parts, which he determines to be antithetical to a formal ethics, founds a basis for historical responsibility. *It will be judged on its form*. If *rigor mortis* is to be understood as absolute immobility, then Genet is striving for an ethics of deadliness in which the formal structure of (theatrical) architecture inescapably implements this injunction. Hervé Guibert's journals, which assume the structure of a mausoleum populated with lovers, transform the responsibility to deteriorating vital impulses into morbid fixity. The undated notes in these pages, recorded over a too-brief decade and a half (1976–1991), foreground, as elsewhere in Guibert's work, a preoccupation with death's vernacular and its attendant familiars—phantoms, shrouds, corpses, and the like. They demand to be read as instantiations of desire, which is to say as an exigent force of vitality, rather than a want for literalised mortification ; the *morgue* in Guibert's phantasm is an expedient textual goad, not a remote foreclosure.

While the body, for Guibert, functions as a theatre of the catastrophal—*reiterating* (without being repetitive) instances of desire—its supplicated other exists in the insatiate epoch of the photographic *instantané*, or momental photo—the *event of light*, in Guibert's semantic—which wishes to absolve itself of subjectivity.

L'ami, an equivocal substantive in French, tending at once toward friend and lover, figures prominently in both the caustic novel, *À l'ami qui ne m'a pas sauvé la vie*, in which Guibert wrote unapologetically of living with the AIDS virus, and as the title of a much discussed black-and-white photograph taken in 1980, in which an arm (the photographer's), outstretched, and visible to the camera, presses against a bare chest, suggesting intimate resistance, figuring the real distance from the aperture to the desired lover, and the vulnerable authority of seeing, a sensuous *mise en abyme* of being seen. Guibert insists, in *Le seul visage : Je crois que mon cas, dans la photographie, n'a d'intérêt que dans ma résistance à la photographie...*[2] Guibert's resistance is twain with an avowed duplicity, a duplicity that is already present in the disjunction

---

[2] *I think that my case, in photography, is only significant for my resistance to photography...*

between his writing, which he characterises as unbridled, and without scruples ; and his photography, with its share of constraint (limited, for example, to instances proffered by travel, by multiple elsewheres)—contrary and *rapt*.

With an eye to obsolescent acception, *rapt* is photography's behest. Already in the photographic *prise* (or *take*), there is the simultaneous suggestion of sexual predation and theft, [3] such that the gesture, interpretable as offering, is not ever altruistic. There is cruelty in it ; the *prise* is a solipsistic act of vandalism ; the catch, of course, is in the inescapability of the subject's subjection to his own motives. Why belabour the point of seeing?

Le mausolée's spur is epistolary. As with Guibert's novel, *L'image fantôme*, in which T. figures both in the dedication, as a refugee from the *roman général*, and in the text itself, *Le mausolée des amants* is first imagined as an open letter to T., Hervé's quintessential *ami*. If Genet has been called up in

---

[3] Evidenced, for example, in the penultimate entry in *L'image fantôme*, "L'image cancéreuse" (The Cancerous Image), in which the narrator, Guibert's double, purloins a photograph of a young man only to chart its untimely degradation, the final stages of which release the imprint into Guibert's covetous skin.

this conversation, just as Hermann Ungar, Franz Kafka, Peter Handke, or Thomas Bernhard might be, it is with a precise dialogic inflection in mind. The usual reliance on lineage as determining for establishing *relations* between texts and at times their authors is undercut by the journal's—and Guibert's—anticipatory attentiveness to extinction. If the work presents itself as a novel *avant la lettre*, it is consigned, by its very writing, to a mode of apprehension ; the low, inescapable pall, of *having been*. Guibert is burying himself, alive. Not *after*, but *with*. Thus are the voices gathered by his pen conversant with, and not precursors to, his vigilous phantasm, permanently eradicating the text's time signature (note, for example, the conspicuous absence of dates on the individual entries).

*

Toward the end of *L'image fantôme*, [4] the question, *Pourquoi m'as-tu tant photographié?* [5]

---

[4] In English as *Ghost Image*, tr. Robert Bononno. Curiously, the English translation removes some of the section titles in the French supplanting them with grafts from the first line of the texts ; one imagines this is to institute a distinction between dialogical entries and narrative ones—a distinction Guibert didn't care to mark—and regrets such efforts, common enough among English language translations, toward systemic redress of perceived inconsistencies in a work.

receives this reply : *Je n'ai pas l'impression de t'avoir beaucoup photographié. Je t'ai certainement moins photographié que je n'en ai eu envie. Je ne sais d'ailleurs pas pourquoi je te photographie… peut-être parce que je ne peux pas te caresser…* [6] *L'image fantôme* is a photographic pretext, a textual photograph, in which no actual photos appear. A scripting of *le désespoir de l'image*, [7] it invokes an intimate amnesia, the perennial obverse of the photograph's destruction of memory. Enlarging this photographic tendency, with epistolary intent, *Le mausolée des amants* is a persistent tender toward that which, imminently, escapes it : a present, with its foregone proximities.

September 2012

---

[5] *Why did you photograph me so much?*

[6] *I don't have the impression that I photographed you a great deal. I certainly photographed you less than I would have liked. I don't really know why I photograph you… maybe because I can't caress you…*

[7] *the despair of the image*

Enculer (footnote)

[1] *Fuck*, here, translates, albeit inadequately, the French *enculer*, which is to bugger. The French refines fucking (*baiser*) to denote specifically *fucking in the ass*, an expression, though legible to an American readership, which takes the form in English of a disparagement, in addition to lacking the economy of *enculer*. Though French does employ the word *enculer* in expressions such as *va te faire enculer* (go get fucked—in the ass), or in the insult *enculé !* (asshole) it retains a literary quality which American English, to my knowledge, does not possess. The British *bugger*, though appropriate, like the *bog* used to designate an American *john* sounds forced, affected, and deprives the passage here, and Guibert's text more generally, of its poetic register, risking reducing the account of a (textually) considered act to a farce. *Fuck*, as an albeit imperfect choice, makes legible the text's intent, and through repetition (eight times here in a 450-word paragraph), I hope, accrues meanings along with the bodies it designates as consummately desired, and *amorously* unspent.

"We are nothing for each other"
(Asphyxia)

No confíes en mis fotos.[1]

—Alejandra Pizarnik

---

[1] *Don't trust my photos.* Tr. Carlotta Caulfield.

In an essay on national feeling published in
1921, Robert Musil identifies pronominal
vacuity thus : "The true 'we'," he writes,
"is : We are nothing for each other". It
is this nothing which is of particular
concern to me, today—now. I would
like to propose now—this moment—as a
nominal now. I am prepared to misspeak
terribly. One of the rare acceptions of

the word "nothing" in the phrase "of nothing"
is "of no account". To Musil's "we" I would
misattribute unaccountability, on account of
this "of no account". If an account is a telling,
a reckoning, a narrative, then this "we" has no
narrative that can be returned to, it hasn't the
value of a narrative, it is without antecedent ;
leaving aside the determination of such value
and the parameters of such a narrative—"we"
may never come to a consensus on such a
thing. Perhaps, if I may speak in broad terms,
if the present is to exceed itself (in language,
say), it must be un-accountable. Least of all to
itself. This may seem a gross prognostication,
and syntactically indefensible. The inevitable
inclination toward pronominality points
precisely to this silence to which one might
be reduced, because it undermines even the
strictures of its own articulation. This is a
chance to take, even as Roberto Bolaño, in
a discussion of Chilean photographer Sergio
Larraín, instructs as to the infernal qualities
of chance—"as if chance were the essence of
hell, its inner workings, its walls, its holes that
swell like eyes." To be nothing for each other
is the zero degree of address, and eventually, of
accountability. Amid the scrawl and spew of
days, there is an argument to be made for the

real. It is made persistently, repeatedly, and with great consequence misapprehended, defended, subdued and upheld. I haven't the luxury of such determination, but I did have in mind something Michelangelo Antonioni discovered in the process of making films, which is that "by submitting the exposed film to a determined procedure known as 'latensification', it is possible to bring out elements of the image which the normal development process is incapable of revealing."

§

This "nothing," I would like to hazard, is the condition of a kind of translation which has become a persistent preoccupation. It is no secret (to myself, I mean), that in recent years, a kind of German toil, has attempted to insert itself, somewhat infectiously, into my unwitting vocabularies. Of this, I can only speak ill, and with little fluency. All of it escapes me in the way one might escape an accident, by hellish chance or determination ; in either case, rashly. These seemed the conditions appropriately suited to a digression into problems occasioned by moments of distraction. Such as this one, in which we meet, over several languages, and driven into the distances prescribed by something which wills itself a now to which none may grant convincing coordinates, and each by his or her pronominal nullity, may claim with any degree of certainty to having attended, for a time, to a number (not necessarily serial) of more or less demanding considerations, the moment of one's own pronominal apprehension having evacuated itself in the very voice by which it is pronounced, mispronounced, delivered, exhausted. In any case, the result is almost always a vertiginous sense of horror, and one need only sample the writings of William Shakespeare or Racine through Martin Buber or James Baldwin, Danielle Collobert or Alejandra Pizarnik, etc. etc., to be convinced of this, on into the dictatorships of Europe and South America, to name but these, past the genocides and philosophies, all the way into this criminally misguided present for a chilling corroboration not only of one's current state of extinction, but of one's untempered ability to anticipate it as well. Admittedly, a consequence of this temporality may be an inability to speak ; simply, whom or what might one be addressing?

I'd like to return for a moment to Musil. In a text first published in a journal in 1913, and included in his *Posthumous Papers of a Living*

Author, translated by Peter Wortsman, Musil recounts in microscopic detail the various deaths observable under a magnifying glass of a population of unwitting flies having come into contact with Tangle-foot brand flypaper, manufactured in Canada. The paper in question supplants the eventual referent of an invisible and irreducible executioner ; it is metonymically amputated. "A nothing, an it, draws them in." Philippe Jaccottet's translation opts for a slower cadence: "Ce n'est pas quelqu'un, c'est cela, c'est 'rien' qui tire sur elles." Returned to English, this translation might read: "It isn't someone, it is it, it's 'nothing' pulling at them." The mortific force in question, the killing spree, say, imputed to the paper, has loosened itself from its anterior hold, from an un-accountable *someone* ": so slowly that one can hardly follow, and usually with an abrupt acceleration at the very end, when the last inner breakdown overcomes them." I might want to introduce here a most telling discrepancy between the English and French translations of Hermann Broch's novel *The Guiltless—Die Schuldlosen*—which arrived in French, unreadably, as *Les irresponsables*: the irresponsible ones. Translation, you see, is its own tribunal, and the gavel falls with the strike of each obsolescent key. Musil's *nothing* is not the smug existent absolved of the world by which it proposes to articulate itself, an unspeaking nether person, as it were, bereft, and thus, free ; rather, it is a nothing replete with inadmissibility. With Musil, we might say: "Let us consider this 'it'."

§

At the very last of *Franza* by Ingeborg Bachmann, the unfinished, and incomplete, second novel in the trilogy of works that includes *Malina* and *Requiem for Fanny Goldman*, each of which is inscribed in the *Todesarten* cycle referred to variously in English as "Death Styles," "Manners of Death," "Ways of Dying," etc., one arrives at a question which determines itself to be insurmountable. Let me first say, with regard to this work, translated into English by Peter Filkins and into French by Miguel Couffon, that in its truncated life, it has existed under several titles already, which bear mentioning, since they manage, through translational and editorial divergence, to split the ear of the text, itself a kind of scream rent from the wound of the literature to which one may wish to bequeath oneself. *Das Buch Franza* (The Book of Franza), which appears elsewhere in Bachmann's notes under the since determined to be provisional title, *Der Fall Franza* (Franza's Case), teeters undecidedly between these qualifiers, arriving in French, decapitated of either its biblical or its psychoanalytic, referent, one might say, since *Franza*, with neither book nor case, captures precisely what I might be meaning by a nominal now, having been robbed of the prepositional clause through which the name—which in French is also a noun—and the person possibly attached to it, arrives. I have found no explanation for the ablation of part of the French title, but I do refer you to a brief passage at the beginning of *Franza*, shall we say, which may render the question moot, inasmuch as the *recognizability* of language—or a thing—is mutely called into question: "Yet as far as we're concerned the train can travel on, for what is written about it will be spoken, the train will travel on, since it is asserted that it exists. For the facts that make the world real—these depend on the unreal in order to be recognized by it."

My argument with the English translation is a simple one: in the cretinous interest of read-ability, and, I can only suspect, a conviction, expressed by so many publishers, of the stupidity of Anglophone readers, the version of *Das Buch*

Franza to which Bachmann's English-speaking
lectorate is relegated is a version rendered
complete by its translator, which is to say, that
unlike the German and French editions (the
only other two versions to which I currently
have remote access), many of the passages of
which are followed by ellipses indicating illeg-
ibility or incompleteness in the author's manuscript, we are given, in the place of Bachmann's
gaping text, something, in English, which
resembles a finished thing, thus promulgating a
fantasy of post-mortal resolution instead of
placing us before the stinking, bloated cadaver,
one which, I might add, one may be equally
capable of loving. Death has its seductions. And
what is death if not the stuff of literature. Of
course the post-mortal moment into which this
nominal now is prolonged has revealed its un-
accountable origins to be murderous. Bachmann
was convinced of this, the demonstrations, now
legion, need not be belaboured.

Leaving aside the disgruntlement occasioned by
versions, there remains the question of the last
sentence of the work, out of which arises the
question of *vollkommen*. The word appears at
the end of the last sentence of *Das Buch Franza*,
which is allocated to the last page of the book,

and falls, in the German edition of volume 2 of the »*Todesarten*«-*Projekt* on page 333, some two hundred pages before the actual end of the book, if one may speak in such terms. The disjunctions here seem to propagate themselves without much effort, as will soon be made evident. It is crucial to bear in mind that the critical edition of *Das Buch Franza* published in German under the direction of Monika Albrecht and Dirk Göttsche does not offer a definitive version of the work any more than do the so-called translations as its determination to reproduce Bachman's work-in-progress makes it replete with indecision, further complicating the translingual quandary (it might be good here to recall the much mishandled archive of one of Bachmann's avowed predecessors in letters, Ludwig Wittgenstein, for a hyperbolic exemplar of the kinds of nefarious departures that can embed themselves in a canonised work mediated by languages that are inherently exiguous to it). When submitted to an international committee of unwitting Germanists comprised exclusively of friends lavishly willing to indulge my desire to see this experiment to its inconclusive end, the word *vollkommen* produced an array of translations, the composite of which manifested in me a kind of sonorous haze, disallowing a decisive rendering of what is proving to be a most confounding sentence. There is no decisive moment in translation, however much its processes may be akin to those of photography. (But Cartier-Bresson's *decisive moment* was of a similar ken to Picasso's *find* ; it is the arrogant articulation of a kind of agonic ecstasy which disallows *erring*.) The fault of translation lies always with the translator. (A lapsus introduced itself into the initial writing of this text, whereupon the prior sentence revealed itself thus: The fault of translation lies always with the translation. I offer it to your scrutiny as precisely the kind of latency by which an aspect of the real may determine to show itself. But one would have to understand language's relationship to the so-called real, and I have yet to be convinced of a reliable conduit, and I have no desire for consensus).

The belated arrival, then, of *vollkommen* into English as *absolute* and into French as *parfait* signals an immediate discrepancy, even to an illiterate eye such as mine. A dictionary proposes: *complete*. The committee has not yet adjourned ; these notes are culled from a still undergoing inquiry. The itineraries proposed by either published translation are potentially incompatible, each is eventually defensible, none may account

for the density of the uncommon *vollkommen*.
Absolute is the most interpretive translation,
parfait remains closest, but lacks the acceptation
of completeness. *Vollkommen* takes its leave of
the sentence in perfect obscurity. It would be
necessary, here, to delve into the middle clause,
which is, by all accounts, quite unwieldy, as
evidenced here by the extraordinary divergence
between the English *after all* and the French *il
faut leur accorder cela*. As to the consequences
and qualities of the Egyptian darkness, now
drained of Franza's person, now suffused with it,
those will have to wait. *Die aëgyptische Finsternis,
das muß einer ihr lassen, ist vollkommen*. The
Egyptian darkness, after all, is absolute. Or, if
you prefer, *Les ténèbres égyptiennes, il faut leur
accorder cela, sont parfaites*. Neither will do, of
course, and this is the plight of any translation ;
however, there is decisional disquiet in this English
after all, which grants the sentence a smugness
it does not itself declare ; and as awkward, at
times, as is the French, in which the darkness is
rendered plural, the confounding middle clause
suggests surrender, which is consonant with the
text's grievous end. I would add, here, perhaps
too hastily, because there is much more to be
said about these divergences which produce in
me an array of discordances, rendering the text

near unreadable (much, as some time ago, I was unable to listen to a public performance of Shostakovich's quartets numbered 7, 9 and 10, precisely because of the subtle and at times less subtle agitation not only of the musicians but of the spectators in their less than accommodating chairs), that though the sentence delivered to Bachmann's readers in English remains, for me, unassimilable, there is something residual in this *after all* which wants, it seems, to wrest mortality from the text, because, as with so many translations, it evidences what amounts to a struggle with a work, and to the death.

§

In 1981, six years after Shostakovich's death by asphyxia, Aleksandr Sokurov agreed to compose with Semyon Aranovich, a film addressing the late composer, through a narratively opaque sequence of discordant clippings and documentary newsreels, all of which inscribed under the rubric of Shostakovich's last composition, the Sonata for Viola, opus 147. The relay between the stern and rigid torso of Evgeni Mravinsky and the frenetic body of Leonard Bernstein conducting the same pounding Symphony No. 5, *Allegro non troppo*, resorts to a whirlingly nauseating reprisal

of the filmmaker's grief-stricken afterness.
Shostakovich once dedicated a quartet to himself, convinced that no one else ever would.
The same quartet was concurrently dedicated
to the victims of fascism and war, perhaps inter-
changeable with himself, and coincident with
the loss of muscular assurance in his hand ; what
would later declare itself to be poliomyelitis, and
destroy his ability to perform. In keeping with his
expressed suicidality, the dedication functions as
a kind of promissory afterthought: Shostakovich
imagined the piece as his epitaph. Sokurov's film
closes on a late voice recording of Shostakovich,
lifted by his friend, the violinist David Oistrakh
from a telephone line. The voice is suspended
between mechanisms, flown, as it were, from
itself, stolen into the viewer's present.

¿En dónde estoy? asks Pizarnik in *El infierno musical.*
Estoy en un jardín. // Hay un jardín.[2]

One further thing: there is a still photograph by
Sergio Larraín of a flock of pigeons dispersing,
1959, in a London sky. One imagines the distur-
bance that caused their flight. Arrested by the
paper flutter of wings, shreds of atmosphere, one

---

[2] *Where am I? I am in a garden // There is a garden.*

is dangerously rapt. It is a simple lure to ignore that the capture of this movement holds in it the premonition of their demise. Not because of the rigor mortis occasioned photographically by the stilling of time. But because where birds are not afforded sleep, they die.

§

The procedure of latensification such as Antonioni describes requires prolonged exposure. We know from Czech photographer Josef Koudelka that too long a bath drowns the image altogether. Why this photographic coda? Because the apprehension of the time of which I have been speaking, this nominal now, is the luminant "nothing to ourselves" in which the image we hold for each other is itself (reflexively) reduced to silence.

January 2013

, but the memory of the photograph is predicated on forgetting

, but the memory of the photograph (bis)

The recognition that one is Some One after having been No One is an indisputable disappointment, reiteratively corroborated by the tedium of technology. Not only is No One a fanciful way to disappoint one's own coming to a mitigated self (self mitigated, not only by language and the technologies it furthers and curtails, but by the very self it purports to achieve, its

achievement being foregone by a language that
has no commitment to anything other than the
obliteration* of that which it claims to seize ; to
seize upon). The first

* [The French *oblitérer* is not only concerned with
disappearance, effacement—that is, the removal of
objects, selves, the result of which may be immediate
(annihilation) or progressive (wear)—but with the
affixing of a seal upon a stamp, rendering it obsolete,
unreusable, as it were. It is also, not incidentally,
concerned with the obstruction of orifices. In 1962,
Bertrand Goldschmidt wrote in *L'aventure atomique* :
"August 6, 1945, on the war ship which returned him
to Potsdam, President Truman announced the obliteration of Hiroshima by an atomic bomb equivalent
to twenty thousand tonnes of trinitrotoluene." The
publication year of Goldschmidt's text was coincident with the declaration of Algerian Independence
from France (July 2nd), Adolf Eichmann's hanging
at a prison in Ramla, Israel (May 31st), the crash of
an American Airlines Boeing 707 on take-off from
New York International Airport (March 1st), and
Czechoslovakia's defeat by Brazil at the FIFA World
Cup (June 17th). In 1962, *L'Eclisse* (Michelangelo
Antonioni) was released in Milan, Paris and New
York ; *The Trial* (Orson Welles), *Mama Romma* (Pier
Paolo Pasolini), *The Four Horsemen of the Apocalypse*
(Vincente Minnelli), *Vivre sa vie* (Jean-Luc Godard),
Il Gattopardo (Luchino Visconti), *The Man Who Shot
Liberty Valance* (John Ford), and *La jetée* (Chris Marker)
all arrived on the cinematographic scene well.
The deaths of William Faulkner, Georges Bataille,
Yves Klein, John Steinbeck and Marilyn Monroe,
e.e. cummings, Vita Sackville-West, and Candido
Portinari were registered the same year. All of which
coincided with the composition by Iannis Xenakis of
Stratégie, for eighty-two musicians—two orchestras and
two conductors, whereas in March Danielle Collobert

completed, in Italian exile, the writing of *Meurtre*
and Alejandra Pizarnik published *Árbol de Diana*. The
year ended, in Sonallah Ibrahim's *Notes from Prison*,
December, Cairo, with this sentence: "The mouth, like
the prison, contains, when closed, living things."]

identifiable flaw is temporal, since the likely
antagonistic relationship between one's Some
One and one's No One provokes a miserabilist
mise en abyme which undercuts the temporal
niceties of historical linearity, the condition of
the one being quite the condition of the other,
the twain effect of which is the precise effacement
of immediate concern. It may have been evidence
of this which prompted the couthless jeers at
the 1960 screening at Cannes of Antonioni's
L'avventura [...]

*

, but the memory of the photograph is predicated
on forgetting, a sensual necessity. Take, for
example, Pierre Leprohon's assertion that
"L'oubli* ne tue pas seulement celui qui oublie,
mais aussi l'oublié." Already he is speaking in
photographs. The photographs arrive as letters,
and they are illegible. This is not light writing in
a Glashaus, but muddy, crude, untempered
inscription. "Oblivion* does not kill the one who
forgets, but also the one who is forgotten."

What distance is the movement between "L'oubli" and "Oblivion" predicated upon? Traduced, the English sentence abandons its repetitions— *l'oubli, oublie, l'oublié*—for murderous affiliation, the bond between *oblivion* and *kill* exceeding the lapidary eradication of memory, a memory however, which may concomitantly be understood, though only if pressed, to be amorous, for the repetitions of *l'oubli* could evoke echoes of *ljubja*, love. What might love have to do with forgetting? It may be one of its most unreasonable conditions, if the photograph has anything to do with it. In this instance, with its forcibly juridical affiliations, it is English which has staged something of an omission (anticipated by the French), which ceases to be audible in any language, however much it seals the text of the photograph, placing it dutifully under *haus* arrest.

Language, is here, and of necessity, a disappointed* lover. Disappointed by desire?

> * ["We would not be erotic, in other words sick with Eros, if Eros were sound, and by sound I intend just, (adjusted) to man's measure and condition."
> —Michelangelo Antonioni]

Itself also a disappointment. If one admits to lingering, for a time, over an obsolescent acceptation which etymologises disappointment's dispossession, its destruction. We are here in the midst of ill-intended geographies. Imitating the Baroque gestures of the drowned of Malraux's ulterior cinematographic premonition.

*

Perhaps I shall call Rimbaud to the keep after all. In 1862, two half centuries before the afore annotated almanac, one notoriously other to him- so-called self, and belated gun-runner, entered middle school, some eleven years before publishing, at his own expense, *Une saison en enfer*, the first line of which, while already cited *ad nauseam* and no doubt to ill effect, stages the unmaking precisely of that which falls under the purview of memory, of memory's own *Jadis, si je me souviens bien*— an avowal of memory's loss if ever there was one, cast against centuries (it seems) of ill-mannered letters, and spoliated by unwarranted repetitions. When David Wojnarowicz takes Rimbaud, so to speak, in (to) New York, it is precisely out of this spent memory that he stages the death pangs of an over-written poet in the embrace of an excessively photographed city, replete with its more and less crude positionings, in the throes of photographic indecency itself.

It is memory, of course, that is indecent, as indecent as Rimbaud's excoriated beauty, and as diminished as the dilapidated buildings of Wojnarowicz's incumbent remembrance. He gives "man's measure and condition" to the photograph and discovers it to be rot ; which is to say, vital, and unapprehendable in its vitality, bug-ridden, and mildewed, and feverish and foregone. What memory he inscribes is the memory of a disappointment, a disappointed memory, trounced, and tyrannical, with a flair for murder and forgetting, *mea mea*.

*

Memory is nothing other than language's obturator. Where it lets light pass, it blinds. Where it opens, it obstructs. When, in 1945, André Bazin affirms "D'autre part le cinéma est un language", in riposte to another André—Malraux's—assertion that "Par ailleurs, le cinéma est une industrie" (1939), bracketing the Second World War with two of the twentieth century's salient concerns—language and capital technology—the temptation is strong to locate in these intended conflictual observations a lapse contending commodified seriation. Why would that not provoke a disappointment? And how

might language be both a disappointment (which
is to say anachronistically slewn and revived,
and slewn again), and induce, while forestalling
it, disappointment's disappointment—Some One's
No One's Some One, as it were? For language is
the obliviated bed in which memory lies, and it
takes its prevaricating pleasures there, in the grain
of forgotten—of forgetting—photographs.

March 2013

Exulant, or The Rain

I cannot seriously suppose that I am at this moment dreaming. Someone who, dreaming, says 'I am dreaming', even if he speaks audibly in doing so, is no more right than if he said in his dream 'it is raining', while it was in fact raining. Even if his dream were actually connected with the noise of the rain.

—Ludwig Wittgenstein
tr. *Denis Paul and*
G.E.M. Anscombe

: Let's listen to the rain and what we say about it.
—Jacques Derrida
tr. *Jeff Fort*

(1965 : 1956)
In the second consecutive chapter of *A Lua Vem da Ásia* (The Moon Comes from Asia) by Campos de Carvalho, which is in fact numbered 18, the eighteenth chapter, much as one might find such a designation on a map, a map, say of Paris, with its Eighteenth Arrondissement, its north end, as it were, with its Gare du Nord and its open-air

markets, and clustered populations, bakeries and 1980s bombings, its Marcadet-Poissonniers métro station, and its sparrows in someone's memory, murdered by the French feet of a passer-by, all of which in a substitutive souvenir, which is not Campos de Carvalho's, who published *A Lua* in 1965 [1], between the Algerian uprising, France's shame and May '68, its solicited acquittal from a Gaullist fantasy, coincident with Ato Institucional Número Cinco—AI-5 under Brazil's military dictatorship, the reader of *A Lua* is presented with ample evidence, in the form of the narrator's imaginary, as to silence's complicity with imbecility: "If I cried out, it is possible that the rain would continue to fall, but the silence, at least, would cease to exist in my room and in the adjoining rooms and the rain would no longer have to beat the unanimous measure of the slumber of all the imbeciles on earth."

---

[1] *A Lua* was in fact published in 1956, a fact that escaped the proofreaders of the 1976 French translation by Alice Raillard published by Albin Michel. What does it matter, anyway, whether the work first manifested itself just as Brasília was being planned and developed or whether it was surmised in the midst of post-colonial insurrection? For myself, I shall prefer the number sixty-five for its historical impertinence. *Errare*, n'est-ce pas? Certainly, this dyslexic accident has thrown thought out of its well-worn habits.

(1795)

Nürtingen, near Stuttgart, 4 September 1795: In an oft-cited letter from one Friedrich to another, Hölderlin invokes to Schiller his intimate condition as an exile, likening himself to a tarnished mirror, accusing himself of inhibiting reciprocity. Hölderlin's denunciation of the "absolute ... *I*, or whatever one wants to call it," the resultant union of subject and object, is negation and proscription, an isn't or am not. In a composite of versions, a strangeness intervenes, echoing Hölderlin's self-recriminations, as though the language itself were held to the impossible task of accounting for its refuted origins: the exile of Jeremy Adler and Charlie Louth's version balking at the unparalleled French, which proffers *le trouble du proscrit* in the place where Hölderlin's castigation of himself as outcast is inscribed, disequilibriating the juxtaposed versions: »Es ist mir oft, wie einem Exulanten.«

(1920s)

To my knowledge, there exists only a single composite photograph by the Viennese philosopher. This one combines four faces— his own, and those of his three sisters. Far from reinforcing the fundamentalism of descendancy through the resemblance of traits, as it is so often argued, this procedure severs the contact with its anterior face. The composite photograph, which is no longer a face, but an image in depth, which both appeals to and belies itself at the same time, attributes to the present the topographic depth which comprises it. Imbued with several blurred pasts, it operates a kind of amnesic gesture which is a property of photography, a gorged present, and whose necessarily disjunct memory, grants its immediacy an amnesic surcharge.

(1976–1983)
During the Guerra Sucia, the word *detención*, denoting waiting, exfoliated its more sinister sense of *arrest*, such that after many years of absence from Argentina, of *exilio*, under the recently defunct Videla, a rare war criminal to have died his last days in solitude in a prison cell, a returning Argentine immediately fled the country at the sight of a bus stop.

Exulanten
The exactitude of Exulanten being untransmittable into either French or English, the

specificity of the singularly *Protestant* acceptation of Exulanten being unreceivable in the available vocabularies of *exile* or *l'exil*, one is propelled into a manifestation perhaps of the correspondence drawn, if only nominally, by Camus in *L'exil ou le royaume*, in which the conjunction keeps distinct what language purports here (the German language) to enmesh, which is a particular value attributed to proscription, the German *Exil* dispensing with the rest, while a happy circumstance of obsolescence indicates a synonymous suggestion in the form of explantation—the *explant* in this instance, one perhaps afflicted, as in Hölderlin's hyperbolic case, with *exilium*, proffers the perhaps elucidating, now refuted, record of waste or devastation, ruin or ravage. What the Old French pronounces as *mettre en essil*—to place in exile—may be less incumbent upon a particularized relationship to a particular place, than it may be to oneself, the unspeakable *I* of Hölderlin's lament, emaciated by the negating, or at very least displacing qualifier, "whatever one wants to call it," calling into question, less the tarnish than the mirror.

The Rain
If this is a trajectory, it is one without proper

indications, for what does it matter whether it is then or now, when memory's conduct is so disorderly? The present is never finished absolving itself. 1957: "No. Non pioverà. È umido. È sempre così la notte." [2] (*Le Notti Bianche*).

Dies Irae

Listening owes much to the mouth, more, perhaps, than to the ear to which it is usually so prosaically ascribed. In Sonallah Ibrahim's prison notebooks, *Yamwiyyât al-Wâhât*, for example, he recognises, December, in the midst of Brecht and Eisenstein, Tvardovsky and Sholokhov, 1962, the Western Desert, that: "The mouth, like the prison, contains, when closed, living things." A clear decade later, the score of Galina Ustvolskaya's *Composition No. 2, "Dies Irae"*, for eight double-basses, percussion and piano, includes among the listed instruments, a "wooden cube". Not so far from the scientist's undecipherable "black box", Ustvolskaya's reverberant instrument, relegated to an unmarked staff and a single

---

[2] *No, it won't rain. It's just damp. It's always like that at night.* Tr. Stephanie Friedman

horizontal line, in the eighty-four-page score,
designates: a coffin. It is assumed to be empty.

The Rain (bis)
It is not raining in the Viennese photograph, not
in any of the faces, but there is the suggestion
of rain, which is the suggestion of a particular
kind of face, modulated, after Francis Galton's
disfiguring photographic processes; in either case
divided, or, perhaps instead, apprehensive of its
inscrutable outcome, Daniel Borzutzky, 2011:
"I let the rain pour over my head and I
wondered who I would be when I came out of
your voice." Explanted into this thinking, the
emancipation from the voice, severed as it must
be from speaking (how else might one *cry out*),
is the very inclination of the photograph to
produce itself posthumously, as a premonition
of some nothing— a historical nothing, with
its falsified transcripts and conspicuously
obliterative evacuations: the photograph,
in this instance, is a voice recording of the
rain in which the I, such as it is smuggled out
of captivity, is bequeathed to the accusation
of its unmarred culpability, tried, and tried
again, doggedly, against national inclemency:
a forensics beholden to no body, rejoindering
eradication.

Sotto la pioggia

There is that moment, in Sokurov's film in homage to Shostakovich, in which the composer is sitting on a train, and the rivulets of water on the window submerge the screen. A harrowing frame. For it is a rendering of the face of the composer.

(1956–1960)

He desatado el corazón de la lluvia [3] There exists a contested etymology of exile which perpetuates the commonly misheld conviction of Exulanten's rootedness in (etymological) soil. When Vittoria, borrowed into the person of Monica Vitti, crosses, 1962, the street, stopping mid-way between the promised kiss and indifference, she is rehearsing the scene of her execution. This is no theatre of exile, the establishment of movements of bodies and continents rehashed by the same expiatory stories, but a theatre of obliteration, inscribed in the very boundary out of which all distances are made, and whose first matter is anachronic. Anachronism of this word, *exile*, out of which so many subjugations are made.

---

[3] Alejandra Pizarnik. *I detached the heart from the rain.*

Cap 110 (1830)
My question, then, is this : when it rains, does it
rain into the mouth of the heart ?

May 2013

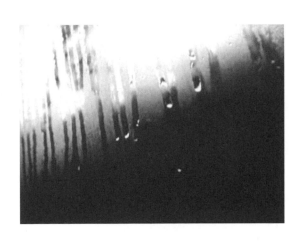

Mein abendes N.

Ich bin noch hungrig.
> —Sigmund Freud to Arnold Zweig
> July 15, 1934

Epic and rhapsodic in the strictest sense,
genuine memory must therefore yield an
image of the person who remembers, in
the same way a good archaeological report
not only informs us about the strata from
which its findings originate, but also gives
an account of the strata which first had to
be broken through.
> —Walter Benjamin
> tr. Edmund Jephcott
> 1932

dans la caméra, j'avais renversé le lit
> —Chantal Neveu
> 2003

∞ It is a quiet disgrace, I think, this speaking.

∞ *The cinema is a calculated deprivation of*
dreaming. A scaling of skins sequencing an
unrecognized city, and the traversal, innumer-
able, of an overpopulated country, cement
buildings, and glass, by which passage, which
undergrowth, by which forbidden way, by
which opening, which kiss in anticipation of a

body, which body drawn into flight, and burning and
futile, which inflammation of the joints and the voices
and the peals and skinning, from tremble to quaking,
nothing ; it says me as though to initiate a rite of re-
nunciation, a vergeless name, a whisper, scarcely, an
asphyxia ; it is neither a desire nor lacking nor even
shame or desistance ; dream it and dreaming, it takes
everything and dies of the clandestinity it prognosti-
cates, the nonetheless of a sexed self, a body without
appearance, birdless, torn, not a name, again, mein
abendes N.; in trespass, it agonies, it was the idea of
an idea that had made me come,

A Star for a Stranger
∞ In a book of unsent letters—unsent because
unreceived—published in German under the title
Wir Eichmannsöhne (We Sons of Eichmann),
German philosopher Günther Anders evokes
the notion of discrepancy (*Diskrepanz*) to describe
one of the Modern conditions necessary for carry-
ing out the *Endlösung* or Final Solution ; *Dis-*
krepanz intends to account for the incoherence,
if I can put it that way, between the machinic
potential proffered by post-industrial technologies, and the human inability to represent to
oneself the final outcomes thereof, in their
totality. This is in the context of an exposé of
not only the grandiose nature of the cogwheel

of the Nazi extermination machine, and Adolf Eichmann's responsibility to and in it *despite* the foreclosure of representation he is faced with, but the larger extent to which the titular "we" (Eichmann's filiates) are implicated in a self-same murderous problematic, such as it is inscribed in the everyday. There are several things to know about Anders, whose work circulates little in English, and poorly at that—and beyond his first matrimonial relationship to Hannah Arendt. This philosopher of obsolescence, whose correspondence with Claude Eatherly, the remorseful reconnaissance pilot who authorized the bombing of Hiroshima, published in English under the title *Burning Conscience*, inscribes the significant anti-atomic effort he exerted after WWII. Anders is also the author of an early polemical work (1934) on Kafka (*pro und contra*), the quality of the English translation of which renders it moot in this language. More significantly, perhaps, for the excavations to be undertaken in your company, today, Anders exchanged names— bartering his bequeathed patronym *Stern* for the more adequate, *Anders*. A star for a stranger. His choice far exceeds the limitations of a *pseudonym* and bears a historical emphasis that can be succinctly corroborated with a few biographical details, all of which involve crossing borders in

Europe and overseas (the United States) to avert
the totalizing outcomes awaiting the majority of
European Jews during WWII.

There is something else in *Wir Eichmannsöhne*
which bears mentioning. The book, such as it is
published, is comprised of two movements. Two
sets of letters addressing Eichmann's son, Klaus,
composed at a twenty-five-year interval, during
which time, Klaus ostensibly made public efforts
to retrieve the purity of his father's so-called
name. These movements, conjugated thus, elicit
their own discrepancy, in time, and in address.
Here, I am tempted to say that these letters are
irretrievable. These are lost letters, buried in a
since-developed compound, and the language
necessary for reading, is lost with them.

It rains since the death of my mother
∞ I would like to say something about the error
of anteriority. Perhaps I can say something
instead about the rain. There is a small book
by Aki Shimazaki the first line of which reads:
"Il pleut depuis la mort de ma mère." If I were
to translate this line grammatically, it might
read: "It has been raining since the death of
my mother." But I would be transposing the
verb tense from the present to a past. A closer
rendering, more accurate, but less *correct*, might

read: "It is raining"—or "it rains"—"since the death of my mother." Beyond the too-obvious correspondence with Camus' now-infamous incipit to *L'étranger*, the temporality produced by this language, as soon as it attempts to exceed itself, is disabled by its own intention. The black rain that fell on Hiroshima within minutes of the bomb blast was produced by a fire-storm. All of this language stands in for a body. A body that is infinitely belated in relation to itself. This is its historical impetus. It arrives before it has arrived. And it leaves after it has left. There is no last, there are only lasts, none of which are lasting. In other words, we are digging up corpses before they are buried. Never mind the dead.

∞ Derrida might offer here an inflection. In the elliptical letters assembled in *La carte postale*, he proposes the following: "Mais je t'écris demain, je le dis toujours au présent." He begins with an objection—*but*—and follows with a temporal admission: *I write you tomorrow, I always say it in the present*. French *admits* this discrepancy, but it does not know that it is doing so. Its fault is in the simultaneity of its condition. In its saying so. Chantal Neveu's *èdres* or hedrons, decapitated polyhedrons, sexed and duplicate, encourage misreading: "je tente de savoir ce qu'il y a avant"—closely, "l attempt to know what there is before." The discord between "there is" and "before" arrests epistemology's claim to an anterior knowledge, or a knowledge of anteriority. What stands in the way is a body. A body in its bed, say, before it hits the floor.

∞ If the voice bequeaths something of a self to a present, it is foremost its discordance. If this is an autobiography, it is both epistolary and photographic, which is to say it is always lying about itself: *I stop, when I stop, and I stop also battering myself, from inside, with my blood, and the unhabitual agreement between time and the world enables me to capture the sonorous aspect of your voice—in other words all of itself, and its sense—your speaking instructs me as to forms of identification which are foreign to me, of identification and of approach, of warmth and of song ; because the voice is an intelligence. You teach me this.*

∞ There is a parenthesis here, a distant shore on which the voices dim beneath the sound of the waves, and detach from their own knowledge.

Something ought to be said about falling
∞ Something ought to be said about falling. It is easy to imagine bodies thrown from a bed, whether or not it is burning. Thrown or thrown

out, expulsed perhaps, the names notwithstanding. Rattling the fire escapes of all the major cities, a kind of photographic mis-coordination. In which the shrieking mouths are fastened shut by the polygraph.

∞ It is tempting, here, to read into the polygraph's cultivated oblivion. From among its several obsolescent acceptations, two offer startling relevancy: the first concerns a person who very closely resembles another—an imitation ; the second, an instrument for graphically recording movements in various parts of the body—what was once termed a myograph, but has fallen out of current usage. But what mouth could account for such a thing? What mouth without a language to obliterate it?

∞ I haven't said I yet, but I soon shall.

∞ By the vagaries of a dictionary, I happen by chance upon these words attributed to an Abbé Chaulieu, who, in an unpublished letter, would have written, in my translation: "My horse falls on me in two instances." It is clear by now that the syntax has exceeded the world it wishes to account for. But I am reluctant to discard these discordances as frivolities or precious attentiveness to exactitude. It is precisely the simultaneity convoked to this experience, the two instances of falling, which disturbs the intricate register of referentiality by which a language lives. If there are two instances of falling, how many selves are fallen upon? It isn't sophistry. Or an ill-educated geometry. But a destructuring accident of the exact sort Goethe was disinclined to attend to in his *Metamorphosis of Plants*. After all, "one doesn't premeditate a photograph," according to Carlo Rim, "like a murder or a work of art." (1930) [1]

∞ There is a concordance here that wants elucidating. *This morning on the train a young man collapsed. He was dead, his eyes open on nothing, dead, his head driven into the seat against which his body had thrown him. Then he got up, angry and ashamed, at having been seen thus to have died by people who certainly hadn't earned the scene of that intimacy.*

∞ Earlier this year, the Musée de la Civilisation de Québec hosted an exhibition of contemporary

---

[1] Tr. Robert Erich Wolf. Carlo Rim itself, is also an annagrammatic *misnomer*, a (literary) derivation from the name ascribed to the author at birth, Jean Marius Richard.

Haitian artworks based on an exhibition held at the Fowler Museum at UCLA in 2012, itself predated by several other related exhibitions. In the promotional materials associated with the Québec exhibition, one is instructed, in French, to "forget the images of natural catastrophe associated with Haiti's poverty and political problems and discover *engagés* artists and their creations in which life and death intermix with disarming derision." Nowhere, in my perusal of the English-language documentation provided by the same museum, or in the material published for the UCLA exhibition, is any such apology made. Fowler, instead, proposes to "explore how leading Haitian visual artists have responded to a tumultuous 21st century, an era punctuated by political upheaval, a cataclysmic earthquake, devastating hurricanes, epidemics, and continuing instability." (This isn't the place to draw out the US influence here on Haiti's reiterated outcomes, nor the UN's introduction in 2010 of a cholera epidemic through poor sanitation practices, nor the euphemised rape of girls by any number of a hundred UN soldiers hurriedly repatriated to Sri Lanka, nor the IMF's abolishment of tariffs in the 1990s resulting in the devastation of Haiti's agriculture). If the pieces given to see have a force of morbid vitality that exceeds the constraints of the museum, what is most strikingly exposed at the Québec exhibition, are the (Cartesian) gallery's own limitations of receptivity to such energies. What is a museum if not a morgue, and which is otherwise mortific: the same. In a manner of falling, the body is steadied against its given name.

∞ "Monstrous," wrote Goethe, "of these rather limited excrescences." [2]

The bed because it is burning
∞ Asclepias are hermaphroditic plants that arrived in Europe from North America, in an inverted traversal: the milkweeds, with their white silks of the seasons and incredulous philosophers. In 1949, the Austrian philosopher himself threw the stems down at his feet in the countryside around Ithaca, declaring them to be: "Impossible !" Does swamp milkweed burn, I wonder.

∞ Asclepias calls in the night. She says there is a fire. The marsh has caught fire, it is said. The marsh catches fire. The house on stilts is progressively gained by the fire. Asclepias

---

[2] Tr. Douglas Miller

doesn't turn a light on. She thinks only to call. Not to cry out. She doesn't cry out, she calls. She takes the telephone to call. Not to cry out. She says that she doesn't have Tityrus's courage. Nor his ability to observe. That all the biological species which will be destroyed by the fire will never have been catalogued. That she will have admired, it's true, the egrets, the frogs, the dragonflies, the lily pads and the silt at the surface of the marsh, but that never will she have arrived at the decision to name them. To attribute to them the name that would be identifiable in a book prepared for that purpose, in other words the identification of species. No more than she was able to name the bird on the island that flew over the poet's house bitten by the sea. It is true, in fact, the traveller's tree was named, but the name itself escapes nomination just as the house will soon escape its structure when it will be gained by the flames. It will be a while yet, several minutes, hours perhaps. Days, if the wind changes direction. Asclepias doesn't count. She calls. She doesn't say to herself that a house made of earth or stone would be preferable to a house on stilts on the verge of catching fire in the marsh. The marsh is far from everything. No place adjoins the marsh. The house and the marsh are one. A single place. A habitation.

An ecosystem. A single call. And a fire. It is
night. Asclepias calls. She doesn't call anyone in
particular. She gives her voice to the telephone.
To the voice that may or may not respond.
Asclepias doesn't try to know whether the other
voice responds. Or even whether there is a voice
other than her own which calls in the night in
flames. The marsh is a place like any other. It
catches fire. It could just as easily have been the
mountain, or the plain. The fire burns wood the
way it burns water. Even stone. The reason for
the fire is immaterial. Asclepias doesn't bother
trying to know where it comes from nor how it
came about. It is there, in the night. Around the
house, and Asclepias, inside, calls.

∞ All this time we have been gathered on the
public square—with its sewers and its grates and
its planted gardens and its footsteps echoing
plutonium. No mention though of its sheep, or
its dreams: "les abîmes si abîme le dernier chant
de la dernière pluie"— [3]

Mein abendes N.
∞ With the night comes evening. I am prepared
now to make an admission. It has no genealogy

---

[3] Rodney Saint Éloi.

or sex. And by now it regards itself as obsolete, with the polygraph that might condemn it. How is it that the Austrian philosopher was willing to give his face to a photograph while refusing to give his voice to a recording? There is an irrefutability of passage in each decision. One of which pulls plants from the hot earth. The other mildews in a poorly ventilated room. A room. Kafka writes, and is translated: "Everyone carries a room about inside him." This text has exceeded the time of translation, with its particular hunger. With the doors flung open, it is always only night, with its glaring sun and the command to speak. With or without a name, the self-sexed body demands to be recognised. Let me add just this. Regarding the "perhaps all too Europeanizing" translation of several leaves of an ancient Chinese manuscript, Kafka once conceded: "It is a fragment. There is no hope of finding the continuation." [4]

∞ In the north-east of Paris, traversed by an obsolete rail line that once marked the perimeter of the city, is a phantasmagoric garden designed by Jean-Pierre Alphand on a site selected under the third Napoléon by the prefect Haussmann

[4] Tr. Ina Pfitzner.

himself (the engineer of urban *éventrement*) ;
before receiving this designation, it was a
gypsum quarry (established after the revolution
and exploited for the new constructions of the
city and for export to America), that doubled as
a stinking dump, where the cut-up carcasses of
horses were disposed of. Prior to the revolution,
back into the fourteenth century, it was land
designated to no purpose other than an occa-
sional gibbet. With little effort, one can extend
this embedded narrative of what is today known
as the Quartier d'Amérique into the (colonial)
traversals that disquiet the official accounts of
nations, with its bodies dredging the rivers and
oceans, and its livid carcasses transcribing lost
memories from out of the atomic sands.

∞ In the middle of last summer, in a closed room
populated by several foreign nationals, I leant
my voice to several languages at once. It was a
wager mitigated by the formality of the occasion
and a lack of available water. Those who weren't
sleeping were stirring their tea. And convul-
sively, we took our clothes off. All of the bodies
were in different stages of decomposition. Here
is what happened: the walls fell out and the sea
rushed in, with its islands, and its detritus. The
public square was built on a certainty embedded

in which is a paradox. The paradox of the agora :
in which the gallows is the condition of democracy.
Freud's *Das Unheimliche* functions as a gauge of
precisely the kinds of historical discrepancies at
work here ; if it wields a mental compass, it is
surely a deregulated compass, its own polygraph,
since it lies as to its directionality. A brief survey
of translingual equivalency reveals a functional
instability. What English proffers as *the uncanny*
with its subsequently proposed *unhomely* corrective,
the French splits along several lines—*l'inquiétante
familiarité*, *l'étrange familiar*, *les démons familiers*—
before agreeing (with itself) upon *l'inquiétante
étrangeté* producing a rich corpus of literary
references that disappear in their movement into
other languages ; finally, Italian produces from
out of *Das Unheimliche* the extraordinary—to
unhabituated ears—*Il perturbante*. It is enough
to want to be lied to.

∞ I stop here, in the infraction of evening.

∞ There is an initial discrepancy. It is in the
nominal letter N. of *mein abendes*. If all this
time I have been writing letters to my other
self—*mein anderes ! N.*—their symptom has been
persistently vesperal: a time lapse such as can
only be produced by a body prepared to receive

itself against time and the languages it is made to speak. *Mein abendes N.* is evening at language, a film study of discrepant time signatures with their misappropriated geographies. A self-sexed soliloquy of wild gardens and devastated means, with its fingers in everything.

∞ What do structures know of their defeat, and what does noise know of its shattering?

∞ A postscript: "The lowercase 'a' at abend is intentional. One of these days my errors will be so deliberate as to go unnoticed even by myself. But it is already done. It is in the manner of being called upon to say *I*"—*wenn der Abend kommt.* [5]

∞ *There is no pleasure at returning. A slight disgust, perhaps, a disappointment. The night, grey, washes out the facades of buildings, the puddles of mud are nowhere contradicted in the reflections of the sky and the splattered glass of front doors reveals a light that is just as grey in the interiors. It isn't a slum, but a wealthy neighbourhood that we are crossing on foot, and the voice, when it dares, collides with dull surfaces ; they aren't in the least threatening, on the contrary, they comply with their function as*

---

[5] Franz Kafka, 1917.

surfaces, without the least sign of resistance. We
carry the luggage so as not to further scrape the
midnight ground, which the disappearing moon does
not illuminate, and even the kick at the front door
of the charmless building toward which we make our
way, barely detaches itself from the wood to make a
sound. An indifferent neighbourhood with no aspira-
tion to clandestinity or suspension. A city, in sum.
A city with no letters, with no destination, where the
body no longer has a sense of desire or dislocation.
Where every direction is a form of quiet obedience
to no law. And the trees grow, always higher, before
being cut. When I look out through the window at
the street, it's my face, already, which has thrown
itself down.

∞ This is where the voice is cut. There are the
days since, a fall against the cement, a body
furled in the midst of the shrieking city. How
can such a short distance gather such pain into
a body? With the rush of the fall come the rushes
of an unmade film, tendered by a voice that
doesn't yet know itself to be a voice, already.

May 2014

Postscript
A Short Film On Fascism

La vraie manière d'écrire est d'écrire
comme on traduit. Quand on traduit
un texte écrit en langue étrangère, on
ne cherche pas à y ajouter ; on met au
contraire un scrupule religieux à ne rien
ajouter. C'est ainsi qu'il faut essayer de
traduire un texte non écrit.

—Simone Weil [1]

L'idée est de briser le réel,

—Antonin Artaud [2]

---

[1] The true manner of writing is to write as one
translates. When one translates a text written in a
foreign language, one doesn't seek to add anything ;
on the contrary one takes religious scruple not to add
anything. This is how one must try to translate an
unwritten text.

[2] The idea is to break the real,

‡ Revolution owes everything to catastrophe.

‡ In 1936 Antonin Artaud wrote several texts and conferences destined to a Mexican public. These texts were grouped together much later under the title *Messages révolutionnaires*, a title indicated to Jean Paulhan by Artaud as early as 1936, and eventually

published by Gallimard in 1971. Among these texts only several of them (very few) reach us in Artaud's language, which is to say texts written and thought by himself, in French. In 1962, already, these same texts—much thought will have been given to this very *same*—were published in Spanish in a volume entitled *México*. Between 1936 and 1971, it happened that the French (said to be: original) version of these writings went astray. Aside from the "Trois con-férences prononcées à l'Université de México" which open the volume (and include a fantastic excoriation of the father in good patriarchal form), as well as the "Deux Notes" that conclude it, all the other pieces present in the book, and which represent sixty-five percent of the volume, arrive translated—*retranscribed*, the reader is told—from the Spanish. The eventuality of their translation had been anticipated by the author, who feared for them such a grafted out-come. It happens that the distinction between *retranscription* and *translation* goes unqualified in the editor's notes. What is to be made, then, of the slide between these two terms. Does recourse to *retranscribe* seek to mask an attempt to attenuate the extinguishment of the fires of the written text, its own extinction? From euphemism to euphemism, the way is mired, such that the reader can only wonder whether Dézon and Sollers, the thus designated *retranscribers*, weren't hearing voices.

‡ The background actor twice tenders her arm to have her blood taken. The first time the blood spurts. The second time, it runs. Twice, then, lies as to sequence and simultaneity. What is given to see, is neither the arm, nor the bloodletting, but a consequence of time. The only take is the one shown.

‡ I am coming to the face. A face that is both substantive and substitutive. The face, for example, of Jeanne d'Arc in Dreyer's film.[3] His only great passion. There exist two negatives of the film, the Oslo negative and the contested Lo Duca negative which for many years supplanted the first, especially overseas. If doubling is an effect, not to say a practice, of the cinema, it is no less true that it enjoys a use that is far

---

[3] Dreyer's title, *Jeanne d'Arc's Lidelse og Død* translates as: Jeanne d'Arc's Suffering and Death. The director's tendered register eschews the religious (and nationalist) frame in favour of an existential arc ; the translated title torques the film's emphasis under pressure, likely, of the French Archdiocese and its threat of censure.

more widespread than is often recognised. In the 1920s it was common practice, for cinematographers, in order not to wear out the negative of the film (which would become increasingly degraded with each development) to place two cameras side by side that filmed, simultaneously, the sequences of a film, with, of course, a slight delay, both machines being incapable of occupying the same space at the same time. This delay is visible in Dreyer, when the Oslo negative is placed next to the Lo Duca negative. If one or the other contest the idea of an originary film (a contestation that is fundamental to photographic film... though susceptible, itself, of being contested), notwithstanding the director's selections, it is no less true that the spectator is persistently afflicted with a kind of double vision. I would like to go so far as to attribute composite characteristics to it, which overlay the faces delivered in close-up to make them into an indefinite (and not eternal) face marking the inscription of pain, the transcription of which is the mark of its irreceivability. Because the doubling which blurs Jeanne d'Arc's face with the monk Massieu's, is assignation to the fall in question. A profoundly atheist fall, and which is owed to a recanted, inaudible, lure.

‡ If the flutter reaches the image in decline,
the body that befalls it is subject to that very
same body's protests. Its ramifications touch the
ground, and are only visible in winter, in the
light of a glacial sun. As for the sea, it isolates
the detail of an intractable ache. It speaks a
skin, into its tear.

‡ The island bird owes everything to its voice.
In 1987, when its call was said to have been
heard for the last time, by human ears, it
was measuring the span of its life against its
receivability. What its voice signalled, by way of
the absence of another voice by which to appeal
to its existence, was the manner of an end. The
bird's name is comprised of four letters of the
Roman alphabet, in a language foreign to
European languages, but equivalent to itself ;
each of these four letters is anticipated by an
inverted apostrophe. What, of extinction, is
death, is it a death. The honeyeater did not lose
its voice, its voice was lost to a lack of hearing.
If the human heard the call sound, it is that
what was being received was destined to an
express elsewhere, identified as a species, and
unintended for such a near ear. An ear so near
as to be haplessly incriminated. For the bird

in question its voice is the mark of its disappearance. It owes its eradicated life to it, perched,
perhaps, on an island stem, fallen from its branch.

‡ Ōʻōʻāʻā.

‡ It rained, this morning, very early, in the night.

July 2014

On Concordance

The desire for concordance isn't a simple
concern for adequation between states
of thought, of languages or of places, and
far from a fanatical suturing of frayed
ends in order to make them into a single
and same existential expanse, fixed or
undifferentiated ; no, concordance, in

the same disagreement owed to the self-same,
if concordance is relay or relation, it is never
sameness, or levelling, or smoothing of breaches,
nor re-covery (of imperfect junctions)—I
am thinking, for example, of the Tanzanian
miners buried alive in a ground excavated to its
marrow and re-covered by the bulldozers of a
Canadian mining company—for a pigeon, so it
is said, is pigeon, whether it flies over the Place
des Martyrs or Hyde Park. Such an exchange
rate is inconceivable by the usual avenues of
knowledge. For whosoever says pigeon says both
pigeon and pigeon ! If concordance is a possible
relay between two dissimilars, between bodies
shared by a same word, it is that through it the
disagreement extends to its misunderstanding, in
other words it refers to its self-same dispersions.

The sum of which remarks might come to
mean: *equals doesn't always equal equals.* Though
this creates a mathematically untenable instability,
I would nonetheless argue in favour of translation,
as, say, a poetics of *equivocation* rather than
equivalency.

First delivered as a talk at the Denver edition
of AWP in April 2010, under the erudite
auspices of John Keene and with co-discussant
Timothy Liu, in the context of a panel on
queer translation, **(Self-)translation: An
expropriation of intimacies** was also the
object of a keynote lecture given, in a French
iteration, at l'École Normale Supérieure de
Lyon, a clear year later, in April 2011, on the
occasion of a day of transdisciplinary study of
questions raised by Nathanaël's work, organised
under the astute direction of Myriam Suchet.
The French take of this talk, **Traduction (soi-)
disant: une expropriation d'intimités** was
published in January 2013 by *La vie manifeste* in
Marseille, at the impetus of Amandine André.
Timothy Liu received the English version in
The Lavender Issue of *phati'tude* (2012).

Vigilous, Reel: Desire (a)s accusation was
given voice once at Universität Wien, a re-
converted hospital in Vienna, in December
2009, beneath an icy moon, under Eugen
Banach, Astrid Fellner and Elisabeth Tutschek's
hospitality ; and once more in Small Press
Traffic's Dialogue series in San Francisco's brief
summer of 2010, October. Brian Teare provided
a dwelling for the text in his handheld series of
offcut chapbooks at Albion Press (2010). It was
subsequently published in *Homage to Paul Celan*,
edited by Ilya Kaminsky and G.C. Waldrep.

The tautological tury of a disconsolate mind was first published on *evening will come*, as edited by Joshua Marie Wilkinson.

Reproach, rapprochement was first published in *Asymptote's* October 2011 edition, accompanying an excerpt of a translation by Nathanaël of Hervé Guibert's *Le mausolée des amants*, all under the attentive editorial eye of Florian Duijsens.

Enculer (footnote) is residue from correspondence with Benny Nemerofsky Ramsay following a detailed discussion of the term *enculer* as it appears in Hervé Guibert's *Le mausolée des amants*. The resultant text has taken the form of an on-going print work created by Benny Nemerofsky Ramsay and Alisha Piercy severally posted in sites of erotic potential in Brussels and Berlin. At a conversation at Université de Montréal, conspired by Gail Scott and Robbie Schwartzwald, *enculer's* proposition ignited an excited exchange on the much neglected subject of sodomy. A similar proposal was made at the Conrad Wilde gallery in Tucson at a flash reading invoked by the unrepeatable Samuel Ace. From desert to desert.

"We are nothing for each other" (Asphyxia)'s first word was spoken in camera at an offsite event organised by Judith Goldman on the occasion of a reception at SUNY Buffalo in February 2013. It subsequently arrived in the pages of 58:01 *Chicago Review* under the able editorship of Michael Hansen.

, but the memory of the photograph + , but the memory of the photograph (bis) was commissioned for *Not only this, but "New language beckons us"*, a Visual AIDS exhibition at the Fales Library's Downtown Collection in New York, curated by Andrew Blackley, in which artists and writers were invited to respond to a work from the library archive. The photograph buried in the text, and exhibited on page 83 of this book, is from David Wojnarowicz's *Rimbaud in New York* series.

Exulant, or The Rain through its several iterations has been presented to Francophone publics at Université de Montréal and Université Sorbonne Nouvelle Paris 3, in 2013 and 2014 respectively. The latter occasion inscribed the work in a journée d'études given to the theme 'écritures migrantes des genres' generously attended to by Mireille Calle-Gruber and Myriam Suchet, a subsequent publication of which is imminent with Presses Sorbonne Nouvelle. This marks its first appearance in English.

Mein abendes N. proposed itself as the polygraph keynote lecture for Trish Salah's eminent Writing Trans Genres conference held at the University of Manitoba, Winnipeg, in May 2014.

Postscript: A Short Film On Fascism is a text retranscribed from the French 'Douze chutes d'un film à refaire' published in *Cahiers Artaud* no 2 at Alain Jugnon's editorial behest. Its English double was voiced with some equivocation at the University of Miami at Oxford (Ohio)'s Translation Symposium, September 29, 2014, at Cathy Wagner's generous welcome.

equals doesn't always equal equals

BY THE SAME [sic] AUTHOR

TRANSLATIONS

2014   *The Mausoleum of Lovers*
       by Hervé Guibert

       Je pas je
       by Reginald Gibbons

2013   *Murder*
       by Danielle Collobert

2012   *The Obscene Madame D*
       by Hilda Hilst
       (translated in collaboration with
       Rachel Gontijo Araújo)

2011   *Flowers of Spit*
       by Catherine Mavrikakis

2010   *Poetic Intention*
       by Édouard Glissant

2004   *A Cannibal and Melancholy Mourning,*
       by Catherine Mavrikakis

IMAGES

Cover image Nathanaël: *Paludes*
(b&w photograph) (2014).

28 Claude Cahun: *Que me veux-tu?*
(b&w photograph) (1928).

63 Benny Nemerofsky Ramsay and Alisha Piercy.
Placing the footnote at the Palais de Justice
(colour digital image) (2013), Brussels.
Courtesy of Piercy and Nemerofsky.

83 Contact Sheet; The David Wojnarowicz
Papers; MSS 092; Series XI; Box 44; Fales
Library and Special Collections, New York
University Libraries. Courtesy of the Estate of
David Wojnarowicz.

107 Semyon Aranovich and Aleksandr
Sokurov: *Altovaya sonata* (film still) (1981).

139 Carl Theodor Dreyer: *La Passion de
Jeanne d'Arc* (film stills) (1928).

© 2015 by Nathanaël
All rights reserved
Printed in the United States

ISBN 978–1–937658–39–7

With enduring gratitude to Stephen Motika,
Mark Addison Smith and Nathaniel Feis for
their invaluable assistance in the preparation
of this volume.

Grazie di cuore to Jennifer Scappettone for
passage toward Italian.

Unattributed translations are attributable to
the author.

Design and typesetting
    Mark Addison Smith

Distributed by
    University Press of New England
    One Court Street
    Lebanon, NH 03766
    www.upne.com

    Nightboat Books
    New York
    www.nightboat.org

ABOUT NIGHTBOAT BOOKS

Nightboat Books, a nonprofit organization, seeks to develop audiences for writers whose work resists convention and transcends boundaries. We publish books rich with poignancy, intelligence, and risk. Please visit nightboat.org to learn more about us and how you can support our future publications.

The following individuals have supported the publication of this book. We thank them for their generosity and commitment to the mission of Nightboat Books:

Elizabeth Motika
Benjamin Taylor

In addition, this book has been made possible, in part, by grants from the National Endowment for the Arts and the New York State Council on the Arts Literature Program.

National Endowment for the Arts
arts.gov

State of the Arts

NYSCA